Wedding Readings

G000111926

First published in 2001 by Octopus Publishing Group,
2–4 Heron Quays, London, E14 4JP
www.conran-octopus.co.uk

ISBN 1 84091 229 4

Publishing Director Lorraine Dickey;
Creative Director Leslie Harrington;
Senior Editor Katey Day; *Designer* Megan Smith
Production Director Zoë Fawcett

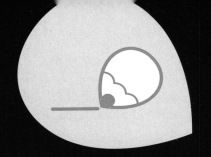

Contents

introduction

Readings can add to the solemnity of an occasion or provide a welcome moment of light relief. At civil weddings, they add colour and individuality to the formulaic; at religious venues, they introduce a breath of worldliness that non-religious people can relate to. Above all, readings emphasize the importance of your day by articulating the values that underlie your momentous decision to marry.

Church weddings

For a religious ceremony, you are usually given a selection of biblical readings, but you may also be allowed to read out a secular text. Exactly how secular the text can be will depend on the church, but perhaps also on the minister. A high Anglican vicar, for instance, might allow some Shakespeare but draw the line at modern poetry, whereas a 'trendy vicar' might consider a much wider selection of texts. Both, however, would want to ensure that the readings do not undermine the Christian view of marriage, so always make sure your choice is approved by the minister or celebrant.

Civil weddings

At a register office wedding, you must obtain prior approval to use any readings. Similarly, in weddings that take place in state-licensed venues, a registrar will need to approve your selection. Remember, too, that civil weddings do not allow for any material with a religious content. Obviously, this rules out biblical texts and hymns, but also more loosely spiritual material, such as *The Prophet*.

If you want more freedom over the content of your marriage service, you might consider an alternative ceremony, such as a humanist wedding. You'll be able to choose from a much greater range of readings, or – if you wish – you may even be able to write your own.

What all good readings have in common is a celebration of married life in all its fullness and variety. The best readings celebrate not just the first flash of passion, but also the enduring qualities of marriage, such as fidelity, security, companionship and mutual fulfilment.

Secular readings

Ideal for civil services, these readings
will also add a note of worldliness
to church ceremonies.

You can give without loving, but you can never love without giving. The great acts of love are done by those who are habitually performing small acts of kindness. We pardon to the extent that we love. Love is knowing that even when you are alone, you will never be lonely again. And great happiness of life is the conviction that we are loved. Loved for ourselves. And even loved in spite of ourselves.

LETTERS TO A YOUNG POET

Rainer Maria Rilke (1875–1926)

For one human being to love another: that is perhaps the most difficult of all tasks, the ultimate task, the final test and proof, the work for which all other work is merely preparation.

Love is at first not anything that means merging, surrendering, and uniting with another (for what purpose would a union of something unclarified serve?), rather it is a high inducement to the individual to ripen, to become something in ourselves, to become a world in ourselves for the sake of another person. Love is a great, demanding claim on us, something that chooses us and calls us to vast distances.

Marriage is in many ways a simplification of life, and it naturally combines the strengths and wills of two young people so that, together, they seem to reach farther into the future than they did before. Above all, marriage is a new task and a new seriousness – a new demand on the strength and generosity of each partner, and a great new danger for both.

The point of marriage is not to create a quick commonality by tearing down all boundaries; on the contrary, a good marriage is one in which each partner appoints the other to be the guardian of his solitude, and thus each shows the other the greatest possible trust. A merging of two people is an impossibility, and where it seems to exist, it is a hemming-in, a mutual consent that robs one party or both parties of their fullest freedom and development. But once the realization is accepted that even between the closest people infinite distances exist, a marvellous living side-by-side can grow up for them, if they succeed in loving the expanse between them, which gives them the possibility of always seeing each other as a whole and before an immense sky.

SONNETS FROM THE PORTUGUESE

Elizabeth Barrett Browning (1806–1861)

If thou must love me, let it be for naught
Except for love's sake only. Do not say,
'I love her for her smile—her look—
   her way
Of speaking gently,—for a trick of thought
That falls in well with mine, and certes
   brought
A sense of pleasant ease on such a day'—
For these things in themselves, Belovèd, may
Be changed, or change for thee,— and love,
   so wrought,

May be unwrought so. Neither love me for
Thine own dear pity's wiping my cheeks
   dry,—
A creature might forget to weep, who bore
Thy comfort long, and lose thy love thereby!
But love me for love's sake, that evermore
Thou mayst love on, through love's eternity.

A BIRTHDAY

Christina G. Rossetti (1830–94)

My heart is like a singing bird
Whose nest is in a watered shoot;
My heart is like an apple tree
Whose boughs are bent with thickset fruit;
My heart is like a rainbow shell
That paddles in a halcyon sea;
My heart is gladder than all these
Because my love is come to me.

Raise me a dais of silk and down;
Hang it with vair and purple dyes;
Carve it in doves and pomegranates,
And peacocks with a hundred eyes;
Work it in gold and silver grapes,
In leaves and silver fleur-de-lys;
Because the birthday of my life
Is come, my love is come to me.

THE PASSIONATE SHEPHERD
TO HIS LOVE

Christopher Marlowe (1564–93)

Come live with me, and be my love,
And we will all the pleasures prove,
That valleys, groves, hills and fields,
Woods, or steepy mountain yields.

And we will sit upon the rocks,
Seeing the shepherds feed their flocks
By shallow rivers, to whose falls
Melodious birds sing madrigals.

And I will make thee beds of roses,
And a thousand fragrant posies,
A cap of flowers, and a kirtle,
Embroid'red all with leaves of myrtle.

A gown made of the finest wool
Which from our pretty lambs we pull,
Fair-lined slippers for the cold,
With buckles of the purest gold.

A belt of straw and ivy-buds,
With coral clasps and amber studs,
And if these pleasures may thee move,
Come live with me, and be my love.

The shepherd swains shall dance and sing
For thy delight each May morning.
If these delights thy mind may move,
Then live with me, and be my love.

FIRST LOVE

John Clare (1793–1864)

I ne'er was struck before that hour
With love so sudden and so sweet
Her face it bloomed like a sweet flower
And stole my heart away complete
My face turned pale a deadly pale
My legs refused to walk away
And when she looked what could I ail
My life and all seemed turned to clay

And then my blood rushed to my face
And took my eyesight quite away
The trees and bushes round the place
Seemed midnight at noon day
I could not see a single thing
Words from my eyes did start
They spoke as chords do from the string
And blood burnt round my heart

Are flowers the winters choice
Is love's bed always snow
She seemed to hear my silent voice
Not loves appeals to know
I never saw so sweet a face
As that I stood before
My heart has left its dwelling place
And can return no more.

Everything that touches us, me and you,
    takes us together like a violin's bow,
    which draws one voice out of two
    separate strings.
Upon what instrument are we two spanned?
And what musician holds us in his hand?
Oh sweetest song.

FORGIVE ME BUT I NEEDS MUST PRESS

Alice Cary (1820–1871)

Forgive me, but I needs must press
One question, since I love you so;
And kiss me, darling, if it's Yes,
And, darling, kiss me if it's No!

It is about our marriage day,
I fain would have it even here;
But kiss me if it's far away,
And, darling, kiss me if it's near!

Ah, by the blushes crowding so
On cheek and brow, 'tis near, I guess;

But, darling, kiss me if it's No,
And kiss me, darling, if it's Yes!

And with what flowers shall you be wed?
With flowers of snow? or flowers of flame?
But be they white, or be they red,
Kiss me, my darling, all the same!

And have you sewed your wedding dress?
Nay, speak not, even to whisper low;
But kiss me, darling, if it's Yes,
And, darling, kiss me if it's No!

A DREAM

Robert C. O. Benjamin (1855–1900)

I dreamed that I loved a sweet maiden,
With hair of bright rippling gold;
And the story I told of my love to her
Is the same one that's ever been told.

I dreamed that her eyes, bright and
    gladsome,
Were dark as the raven's black wing;
And I thought that upon her third finger
I placed a plain gold wedding ring.

I dreamed that her lips, red as cherries,
Were dangerously close to my own;

And the kiss that I gave her whilst dreaming,
Awoke me, so loud was its tone.

But when I awoke I remembered
The cause of my fancy's sweet flight,
And the reason of happy dreaming,
Which made blissful the visions of night.

'Twas a picture which looked from the
    canvas,
Painted though perfect to life,
And so sweet was the face and the tresses,
I dreamed that I made her my wife.

MY LADY LOVE

Robert C. O. Benjamin (1855–1900)

There are none so happy as my love and I,
None so joyous, blythe and free;
The reason is, that I love her,
And the reason is, she loves me.

There are none so sweet as my own fond
    love;
None so beautious or true;
Her equal I could never find,
Though I search the whole world thro'.

There's no love so true as my lady sweet;
None so constant to its troth;
There's naught on earth like her so dear,
No queen her equal in her worth.

So there's none so happy as my love and I;
None so blissful, blythe and free,
And the reason is that I am hers,
And she, in truth, belongs to me.

SONNET NO. 116

William Shakespeare (1564–1616)

Let me not to the marriage of true minds
Admit impediments. Love is not love
Which alters when it alteration finds,
Or bends with the remover to remove:
O, no, it is an ever-fixed mark,
That looks on tempests and is never shaken;
It is the star to every wandering bark,
Whose worth's unknown, although his
   height be taken.

Love's not Time's fool, though rosy lips
  and cheeks
Within his bending sickle's compass come;
Love alters not with his brief hours and
  weeks,
But bears it out even to the edge of doom.
If this be error and upon me proved,
I never writ, nor no man ever loved.

A RED, RED ROSE

Robert Burns (1759–1796)

O my Luve's like a red, red rose,
That's newly sprung in June;
O my Luve's like the melodie
That's sweetly play'd in tune.—

As fair art thou, my bonie lass,
So deep in luve am I;
And I will luve thee still, my Dear,
Till a' the seas gang dry.—

Till a' the seas gang dry, my Dear,
And the rocks melt wi' the sun:
I will luve thee still, my Dear,
While the sands o' life shall run.—

And fare thee weel, my only Luve!
And fare thee weel, a while!
And I will come again, my Luve,
Tho' it were ten thousand mile.—

SONG OF THE OPEN ROAD
Walt Whitman (1819–1892)

Listen! I will be honest with you,
I do not offer the old smooth prizes, but
    offer rough new prizes,
These are the days that must happen
    to you:
You shall not heap up what is call'd riches,
You shall scatter with lavish hand all that
    you earn or achieve.

However sweet these laid-up stores,
    however convenient this dwelling, we
    cannot remain there.

However shelter'd the port, and however
    calm the waters, we must not anchor
    here,
However welcome the hospitality that
    surrounds us we are permitted to receive
    it but a little while.

Afoot and light-hearted I take to the open
    road,
Healthy, free, the world before me,
The long brown path before me leading
    wherever I choose.

Camerado, I give you my hand!
I give you my love more precious than
 money,
I give you myself before preaching or law;
Will you give me yourself? Will you come
 travel with me?
Shall we stick by each other as long as we
 live?

DOVE POEM

Author Unknown

Two doves meeting in the sky
Two loves hand in hand eye to eye
Two parts of a loving whole
Two hearts and a single soul

Two stars shining big and bright
Two fires bringing warmth and light
Two songs played in perfect tune
Two flowers growing into bloom

Two doves gliding in the air
Two loves free without a care
Two parts of a loving whole
Two hearts and a single soul

A GOOD WEDDING CAKE

Author Unknown

4lb of love
½lb of good looks
1lb of sweet temper
1lb of butter of youth
1lb of blindness of faults
1lb of pounded wit
1lb of good humour
2 tablespoons of sweet argument
1 pint of rippling laughter
1 wine glass of common sense
dash of modesty

... good looks and sweet temper
into a we.. .urnished house. Beat the butter
of youth to a cream, and mix well together
with the blindness of faults. Stir the
pounded wit and good humour into the
sweet argument, then add the rippling
laughter and common sense. Add a dash
of modesty and work the whole together
until everything is well mixed. Bake gently
for ever.

ON YOUR WEDDING DAY
Author Unknown

Today is a day you will always remember
The greatest in anyone's life
You'll start off the day just two people
  in love
And end it as Husband and Wife
It's a brand new beginning the start of
  a journey
With moments to cherish and treasure
And although there'll be times when you
  both disagree
These will surely be outweighed by pleasure
You'll have heard many words of advice in
  the past

When the secrets of marriage were spoken
But you know that the answers lie hidden
   inside
Where the bond of true love lies unbroken
So live happy forever as lovers and friends
It's the dawn of a new life for you
As you stand there together with love in
   your eyes
From the moment you whisper 'I do'
And with luck, all your hopes, and your
   dreams can be real
May success find its way to your hearts
Tomorrow can bring you the greatest of joys
But today is the day it all starts.

APACHE BLESSING
Author Unknown

Now you will feel no rain, for each of you will be the shelter for each other. Now you will feel no cold, for each of you will be the warmth for the other. Now you are two persons, but there is only one life before. Go now to your dwelling place to enter into the days of your life together. And may your days be good and long upon the earth.

Treat yourselves and each other with respect, and remind yourselves often of what brought you together. Give the highest priority to the tenderness, gentleness and kindness that your connection deserves. When frustration, difficulty and fear assail your relationship – as they threaten all relationships at one time or another – remember to focus on what is right between you, not only the part which seems wrong. In this way, you can ride out the storms when clouds hide the face of the sun in your lives – remembering that even if you lose sight of it for a moment, the sun is still there. And if each of you takes responsibility for the quality of your life together, it will be marked by abundance and delight.

MARRIED LOVE

Kuan Tao-Sheng (1263–1319)

You and I
Have so much love
That it
Burns like a fire,
In which we bake a lump of clay
Moulded into a figure of you
And a figure of me.
Then we take both of them,
And break them into pieces,

And mix the pieces with water,
And mould again a figure of you,
And a figure of me.
I am in your clay.
You are in my clay.
In life we share a single quilt.
In death we will share one bed.

ESKIMO LOVE SONG
Author Unknown

You are my husband [wife]
My feet shall run because of you
My feet dance because of you
My heart shall beat because of you
My eyes see because of you
My mind thinks because of you
And I shall love because of you.

A CHINESE POEM

Author Unknown

I want to be your friend forever and ever
When the hills are all flat
and the rivers run dry
When the trees blossom in winter
and the snow falls in summer,
when heaven and earth mix —
not till then will I part from you.

Non-secular readings

If you'd like to underline the spiritual element of your marriage, then you might like to include a reading from this selection.

EXTRACT FROM **THE DIVINE COMEDY**
Dante (1265–1321)

The love of God, unutterable and perfect,
flows into a pure soul the way light rushes
into a transparent object. The more love we
receive, the more love we shine forth; so
that, as we grow clear and open, the more
complete the joy of loving is. And the more
souls who resonate together, the greater
the intensity of their love for, mirror-like,
each soul reflects the other.

THE PROPHET

Kahlil Gibran (1883–1931)

Your friend is your needs answered. He is your field which you sow with love and reap with thanksgiving. And he is your board and your fireside. For you come to him with your hunger, and you seek him for peace.

When your friend speaks his mind you fear not the 'nay' in your own mind, nor do you withhold the 'aye'. And when he is silent your heart ceases not to listen to his heart; For without words, in friendship, all thoughts, all desires, all expectations are born and shared, with joy that is unclaimed.

When you part from your friend, you grieve
not; for that which you love most in him
may be clearer in his absence, as the
mountain to the climber is clearer from
the plain.

And let there be no purpose in friendship
save the deepening of the spirit. For love
that seeks aught but the disclosure of its
own mystery is not love but a net cast
forth: and only the unprofitable is caught.

And let your best be for your friend. If he must know the ebb of your tide, let him know its flood also. For what is your friend that you should seek him with hours to kill? Seek him always with hours to live. For it is his to fill your need, but not your emptiness. And in the sweetness of friendship let there be laughter, and sharing of pleasures. For in the dew of little things the heart finds its morning and is refreshed.

ON MARRIAGE

Kahlil Gibran (1883–1931)

Then Almitra spoke again and said, 'And
  what of Marriage, master?'
And he answered saying:
You were born together, and together you
  shall be forevermore.
You shall be together when white wings of
  death scatter your days.
Aye, you shall be together even in the silent
  memory of God.
But let there be spaces in your
  togetherness,
And let the winds of the heavens dance
  between you.

Love one another but make not a bond of
  love:
Let it rather be a moving sea between the
  shores of your souls.
Fill each other's cup but drink not from one
  cup.
Give one another of your bread but eat not
  from the same loaf.
Sing and dance together and be joyous, but
  let each one of you be alone,
Even as the strings of a lute are alone
  though they quiver with the same music.

Give your hearts, but not into each other's
keeping.
For only the hand of Life can contain your
hearts.
And stand together, yet not too near
together:
For the pillars of the temple stand apart,
And the oak tree and the cypress grow not
in each other's shadow.

TO MY DEAR AND LOVING HUSBAND

Anne Bradstreet (c.1612–1672)

If ever two were one, then surely we.
If ever man were lov'd by wife, then thee.
If ever wife was happy in a man,
Compare with me, ye women, if you can.
I prize thy love more than whole Mines of
   gold
Or all the riches that the East doth hold.
My love is such that Rivers cannot quench,
Nor ought but love from thee give
   recompetence.
Thy love is such I can no way repay.
The heavens reward thee manifold, I pray.
Then while we live, in love let's so persever
That when we live no more, we may live ever.

DESTINY

Sir Edwin Arnold (1832–1904)

Somewhere there waiteth in this world
  of ours
For one lone soul another lonely soul,
Each choosing each through all the weary
  hours
And meeting strangely at one sudden goal.
Then blend they, like green leaves with
  golden flowers,
Into one beautiful and perfect whole;
And life's long night is ended, and the way
Lies open onward to eternal day.

TO CELIA

Ben Jonson (1572–1637)

Drink to me, only with thine eyes,
And I will pledge with mine;
Or leave a kisse but in the cup,
And I'll not look for wine.
The thirst that from the soul doth rise,
Doth ask a drink divine;
But might I of Jove's Nectar sup,
I would not change for thine.

I sent thee late a rosie wreath,
Not so much honouring thee,
As giving it a hope, that there
It could not withered bee.
But thou thereon didst only breathe,
And sent'st it back to me;
Since when it grows, and smells, I swear,
Not of itself, but thee.

THE GOOD-MORROW

John Donne (1572–1631)

I wonder by my troth, what thou, and I
Did, till we lov'd? were we not wean'd till
  then?
But suck'd on countrey pleasures, childishly?
Or snorted we in the seven sleepers den?
T'was so; but this, all pleasures fancies bee.
If ever any beauty I did see,
Which I desir'd, and got, t'was but a dreame
  of thee.

And now good morrow to our waking
    soules,
Which watch not one another out of feare;
For love, all love of other sights controules,
And makes one little roome, an every
    where.
Let sea-discoverers to new worlds have
    gone,
Let Maps to other, worlds on worlds have
    showne,
Let us possesse one world, each hath one,
    and is one.

My face in thine eye, thine in mine appeares,
And true plaine hearts doe in the faces rest,
Where can we finde two better
  hemispheares
Without sharpe North, without declining
  West?
What ever dyes, was not mixt equally;
If our two loves be one, or, thou and I
Love so alike, that none doe slacken, none
  can die.

THE NEWLY-WEDDED

Winthrop Mackworth Praed (1802–1839)

Now the rite is duly done;
Now the word is spoken;
And the spell has made us one
Which may ne'er be broken:
Rest we, dearest, in our home,—
Roam we o'er the heather,—
We shall rest, and we shall roam,
Shall we not? together.

From this hour the summer rose
Sweeter breathes to charm us;
From this hour the winter snows
Lighter fall to harm us:
Fair or foul—on land or sea—
Come the wind or weather,
Best and worst, whate'er they be,
We shall share together.

Death, who friend from friend can part,
Brother rend from brother,
Shall but link us, heart and heart,
Closer to each other:
We will call his anger play,
Deem his dart a feather,
When we meet him on our way
Hand in hand together.

LOVE (III)
George Herbert (1593–1633)

Love bade me welcome: yet my soul drew
  back,
Guilty of dust and sin.
But quick-ey'd Love, observing me grow
  slack
From my first entrance in,
Drew nearer to me, sweetly questioning
If I lack'd any thing.

A guest, I answer'd, worthy to be here:
Love said, You shall be he.
I, the unkind, ungrateful? Ah my dear,
I cannot look on thee.

Love took my hand and smiling did reply,
Who made the eyes but I?

Truth, Lord, but I have marr'd them: let my
    shame
Go where it doth deserve.
And know you not, says Love, who bore the
    blame?
My dear, then I will serve.
You must sit down, says Love, and taste my
    meat:
So I did sit and eat.

SONNET NO. 18

William Shakespeare (1564–1616)

Shall I compare thee to a summer's day?
Thou art more lovely and more temperate:
Rough winds do shake the darling buds of
   May,
And summer's lease hath all too short a
   date;
Sometime too hot the eye of heaven shines,
And often is his gold complexion dimm'd;
And every fair from fair sometime declines,
By chance, or nature's changing course,
   untrimm'd.
But thy eternal summer shall not fade,
Nor lose possession of that fair thou owest;

Nor shall Death brag thou wanderest in
   his shade,
When in eternal lines to time thou
   growest;
So long as men can breathe, or eyes can see,
So long lives this, and this gives life to thee.

EXTRACT FROM **FIDELITY**
D.H. Lawrence (1885–1930)

Man and woman are like the earth, that
   brings forth flowers
in summer, and love, but underneath is rock.
Older than flowers, older than ferns, older
   than foraminiferae,
older than plasm altogether is the soul
   underneath.
And when, throughout all the wild chaos
   of love
slowly a gem forms, in the ancient, once-
   more-molten rocks

of two human hearts, two ancient rocks,
a man's heart and a woman's,
that is the crystal of peace, the slow hard
    jewel of trust,
the sapphire of fidelity.
The gem of mutual peace emerging from
    the wild chaos of love.

SONNETS FROM THE PORTUGUESE

Elizabeth Barrett Browning (1806–1861)

How do I love thee? Let me count the ways.
I love thee to the depth and breadth and
  height
My soul can reach, when feeling out of sight
For the ends of Being and ideal Grace.
I love thee to the level of every day's
Most quiet need, by sun and candle light.
I love thee freely, as men strive for Right;
I love thee purely, as they turn from Praise.
I love thee with the passion put to use
In my old griefs, and with my childhood's
  faith.

I love thee with a love I seemed to lose
With my lost saints,—I love thee with the
   breath,
Smiles, tears, of all my life!—and, if God
   choose,
I shall but love thee better after death.

EXTRACT FROM **IMITATIO CHRISTI**
Thomas à Kempis (1379–1471)

Love is a mighty power, a great and
    complete good.
Love alone lightens every burden, and makes
    rough places smooth.
It bears every hardship as though it were
    nothing, and renders all bitterness sweet
    and acceptable.

Nothing is sweeter than love,
Nothing stronger,
Nothing higher,
Nothing wider,
Nothing more pleasant,

Nothing fuller or better in heaven or earth;
　for love is born of God.

Love flies, runs and leaps for joy.
It is free and unrestrained.
Love knows no limits, but ardently
　transcends all bounds.
Love feels no burden, takes no account
　of toil,
Attempts things beyond its strength.

Love sees nothing as impossible,
for it feels able to achieve all things.
It is strange and effective,
while those who lack love faint and fail.

Love is not fickle and sentimental,
nor is it intent on vanities.
Like a living flame and a burning torch,
it surges upward and surely surmounts
   every obstacle.

WEDDING PRAYER

Robert Louis Stevenson (1850–1894)

Lord, behold our family here assembled.
We thank you for this place in which we
  dwell,
for the love that unites us,
for the peace accorded us this day,
for the hope with which we expect the
  morrow,
for the health, the work, the food,
and the bright skies that make our lives
  delightful;
for our friends in all parts of the earth.

Amen

PRAYER

St. Francis of Assisi

Lord, make us instruments of your peace.
Where there is hatred, let us sow love;
Where there is injury, pardon;
Where there is discord, union;
Where there is doubt, faith;
Where there is despair, hope;
Where there is darkness, light;
Where there is sadness, joy;
O Divine Master, Grant that we may not
    so much seek

To be consoled as to console,
To be understood as to understand,
To be loved as to love.
For it is in giving that we receive;
It is in pardoning that we are pardoned;
And it is in dying that we are born to
    eternal life.

Amen

IRISH BLESSING
Author Unknown

May the road rise to meet you,
May the wind be always at your back.
May the sun shine warm upon your face,
The rains fall soft upon your fields.
And until we meet again,
May God hold you in the palm of his hand.

May God be with you and bless you;
May you see your children's children.
May you be poor in misfortune,
Rich in blessings,
May you know nothing but happiness
From this day forward.

May the road rise to meet you
May the wind be always at your back
May the warm rays of sun fall upon
   your home
And may the hand of a friend always be near.

May green be the grass you walk on,
May blue be the skies above you,
May pure be the joys that surround you,
May true be the hearts that love you.

HAWAIIAN SONG

Author Unknown

Here all seeking is over.
the lost has been found,
a mate has been found
to share the chills of winter –
now Love asks
that you be united.
Here is a place to rest,
a place to sleep,
a place in heaven.
Now two are becoming one,
the black night is shattered,
the eastern sky grows bright.
At last the great day has come!

TRUE LOVE
Author Unknown

True love is a sacred flame
That burns eternally,
And none can dim its special glow
Or change its destiny.
True love speaks in tender tones
And hears with gentle ear,
True love gives with open heart
And true love conquers fear.
True love makes no harsh demands
It neither rules nor binds,
And true love holds with gentle hands
The hearts that it entwines.

Bible readings

As with all readings and poems that you wish to have read out at your wedding service, you will need to discuss them with your minister first, and obtain his or her approval.

Male and female, He created them.

26 Then God said, 'Let us make man in our image, in our likeness, and let them rule over the fish of the sea and the birds of the air, over the livestock, over all the earth, and over all the creatures that move along the ground.'

27 So God created man in his own image, in the image of God he created him; male and female he created them.

28 God blessed them and said to them, 'Be fruitful and increase in number; fill the earth and subdue it. Rule over the fish of the sea and the birds of the air and over every living creature that moves on the ground.'

20 So the man gave names to all the livestock, the birds of the air and all the beasts of the field. But for Adam no suitable helper was found.

21 So the Lord God caused the man to fall into a deep sleep; and while he was sleeping, he took one of the man's ribs and closed up the place with flesh.

22 Then the Lord God made a woman from the rib he had taken out of the man, and he brought her to the man.

23 The man said, 'This is now bone of my bones and flesh of my flesh; she shall be called "woman", for she was taken out of man.'

24 For this reason a man will leave his father and mother and be united to his wife, and they will become one flesh.

PSALM 67

May God be gracious to us and bless us...

1 May God be gracious to us and bless us
   and make his face shine upon us, Selah

2 that your ways may be known on earth,
   your salvation among all nations.

3 May the peoples praise you, O God; may
   all the peoples praise you.

4 May the nations be glad and sing for joy,
   for you rule the peoples justly and guide
   the nations of the earth. Selah

5 May the peoples praise you, O God; may all the peoples praise you.

6 Then the land will yield its harvest, and God, our God, will bless us.

7 God will bless us, and all the ends of the earth will fear him.

Let us sing to the Lord.

1 Come, let us sing for joy to the Lord;
   let us shout aloud to the Rock of our
   salvation.

2 Let us come before him with
   thanksgiving and extol him with music
   and song.

3 For the Lord is the great God, the great
   King above all gods.

4 In his hand are the depths of the earth,
   and the mountain peaks belong to him.

5 The sea is his, for he made it, and his
   hands formed the dry land.

6 Come, let us bow down in worship, let us kneel before the Lord our Maker;

7 for he is our God and we are the people of his pasture, the flock under his care.

PSALM 100

Make a joyful noise to the Lord.

1 Shout for joy to the Lord, all the earth.
2 Worship the Lord with gladness; come before him with joyful songs.
3 Know that the Lord is God. It is he who made us, and we are his; we are his people, the sheep of his pasture.
4 Enter his gates with thanksgiving and his courts with praise; give thanks to him and praise his name.
5 For the Lord is good and his love endures forever; his faithfulness continues through all generations.

PSALM 121

He will keep your going out and your coming in.

1 I lift up my eyes to the hills— where does my help come from?
2 My help comes from the Lord, the Maker of heaven and earth.
3 He will not let your foot slip— he who watches over you will not slumber;
4 indeed, he who watches over Israel will neither slumber nor sleep.
5 The Lord watches over you— the Lord is your shade at your right hand;
6 the sun will not harm you by day, nor the moon by night.

7 The Lord will keep you from all harm—
   he will watch over your life;
8 the Lord will watch over your coming
   and going both now and forevermore.

PSALM 128

May you see your children's children.

1 Blessed are all who fear the Lord, who walk in his ways.
2 You will eat the fruit of your labour; blessings and prosperity will be yours.
3 Your wife will be like a fruitful vine within your house; your sons will be like olive shoots around your table.
4 Thus is the man blessed who fears the Lord.
5 May the Lord bless you from Zion all the days of your life; may you see the prosperity of Jerusalem,
6 and may you live to see your children's children. Peace be upon Israel.

PROVERBS 31: 10–12, 25–31

A good wife is more precious than jewels.

10 A wife of noble character who can find?
She is worth far more than rubies.

11 Her husband has full confidence in her
and lacks nothing of value.

12 She brings him good, not harm, all the
days of her life.

25 She is clothed with strength and dignity;
she can laugh at the days to come.

26 She speaks with wisdom, and faithful
instruction is on her tongue.

27 She watches over the affairs of her
household and does not eat the bread
of idleness.

28 Her children arise and call her blessed;
   her husband also, and he praises her:
29 'Many women do noble things, but you
   surpass them all.'
30 Charm is deceptive, and beauty is
   fleeting; but a woman who fears the
   Lord is to be praised.
31 Give her the reward she has earned,
   and let her works bring her praise at
   the city gate.

ECCLESIASTES 3: 1–8

For everything there is a season.

1 There is a time for everything, and a
season for every activity under heaven:

2 a time to be born and a time to die,
a time to plant and a time to uproot,

3 a time to kill and a time to heal, a time
to tear down and a time to build,

4 a time to weep and a time to laugh,
a time to mourn and a time to dance,

5 a time to scatter stones and a time to
gather them, a time to embrace and a
time to refrain,

6 a time to search and a time to give up, a time to keep and a time to throw away,

7 a time to tear and a time to mend, a time to be silent and a time to speak,

8 a time to love and a time to hate, a time for war and a time for peace.

Two are better than one.

9 Two are better than one, because they have a good return for their work:

10 If one falls down, his friend can help him up. But pity the man who falls and has no one to help him up!

11 Also, if two lie down together, they will keep warm. But how can one keep warm alone?

12 Though one may be overpowered, two can defend themselves. A cord of three strands is not quickly broken.

MATTHEW 5: 1–10

The Beatitudes.

1 Now when he saw the crowds, he went up on a mountainside and sat down. His disciples came to him,

2 and he began to teach them, saying:

3 'Blessed are the poor in spirit, for theirs is the kingdom of heaven.

4 Blessed are those who mourn, for they will be comforted.

5 Blessed are the meek, for they will inherit the earth.

6 Blessed are those who hunger and thirst for righteousness, for they will be filled.

7 Blessed are the merciful, for they will be shown mercy.

8 Blessed are the pure in heart, for they will see God.

9 Blessed are the peacemakers, for they will be called sons of God.

10 Blessed are those who are persecuted because of righteousness, for theirs is the kingdom of heaven.'

MATTHEW 22: 36–40

The greatest commandment.

36 'Teacher, which is the greatest
   commandment in the Law?'

37 Jesus replied: '"Love the Lord your God
   with all your heart and with all your soul
   and with all your mind."

38 This is the first and greatest
   commandment.

39 And the second is like it: "Love your
   neighbour as yourself."

40 All the Law and the Prophets hang on
   these two commandments.'

*What God has joined together let no man
put asunder.*

6 'But at the beginning of creation God
   "made them male and female".

7 "For this reason a man will leave his
   father and mother and be united to
   his wife,

8 and the two will become one flesh."
   So they are no longer two, but one.

9 Therefore what God has joined
   together, let man not separate.'

Jesus's first miracle at the wedding in Cana.

1 On the third day a wedding took place at Cana in Galilee. Jesus's mother was there,

2 and Jesus and his disciples had also been invited to the wedding.

3 When the wine was gone, Jesus's mother said to him, 'They have no more wine.'

4 'Dear woman, why do you involve me?' Jesus replied. 'My time has not yet come.'

5 His mother said to the servants, 'Do whatever he tells you.'

6 Nearby stood six stone water jars, the kind used by the Jews for ceremonial

washing, each holding from twenty to thirty gallons.

7 Jesus said to the servants, 'Fill the jars with water'; so they filled them to the brim.

8 Then he told them, 'Now draw some out and take it to the master of the banquet.' They did so,

9 and the master of the banquet tasted the water that had been turned into wine. He did not realize where it had come from, though the servants who had drawn the water knew. Then he called the bridegroom aside

10 and said, 'Everyone brings out the choice wine first and then the cheaper wine after the guests have had too much to drink; but you have saved the best till now.'

11 This, the first of his miraculous signs, Jesus performed at Cana in Galilee. He thus revealed his glory, and his disciples put their faith in him.

12 After this he went down to Capernaum with his mother and brothers and his disciples. There they stayed for a few days.

JOHN 15: 1–8

I am the vine and you are the branches.

1 'I am the true vine, and my Father is the gardener.

2 He cuts off every branch in me that bears no fruit, while every branch that does bear fruit he prunes so that it will be even more fruitful.

3 You are already clean because of the word I have spoken to you.

4 Remain in me, and I will remain in you. No branch can bear fruit by itself; it must remain in the vine. Neither can you bear fruit unless you remain in me.

5 'I am the vine; you are the branches. If a man remains in me and I in him, he will bear much fruit; apart from me you can do nothing.

6 If anyone does not remain in me, he is like a branch that is thrown away and withers; such branches are picked up, thrown into the fire and burned.

7 If you remain in me and my words remain in you, ask whatever you wish, and it will be given you.

8 This is to my Father's glory, that you bear much fruit, showing yourselves to be my disciples.'

Love one another as I have loved you.

9 'As the Father has loved me, so have I loved you. Now remain in my love.

10 If you obey my commands, you will remain in my love, just as I have obeyed my Father's commands and remain in his love.

11 I have told you this so that my joy may be in you and that your joy may be complete.

12 My command is this: Love each other as I have loved you.

13 Greater love has no one than this, that he lay down his life for his friends.

14 You are my friends if you do what I command.

15 I no longer call you servants, because a servant does not know his master's business. Instead, I have called you friends, for everything that I learned from my Father I have made known to you.

16 You did not choose me, but I chose you and appointed you to go and bear fruit – fruit that will last. Then the Father will give you whatever you ask in my name.

17 This is my command: Love each other.'

I CORINTHIANS 13: 1–13

The greatest of these is love.

1 If I speak in the tongues of men and of angels, but have not love, I am only a resounding gong or a clanging cymbal.

2 If I have the gift of prophecy and can fathom all mysteries and all knowledge, and if I have a faith that can move mountains, but have not love, I am nothing.

3 If I give all I possess to the poor and surrender my body to the flames, but have not love, I gain nothing.

4 Love is patient, love is kind. It does not envy, it does not boast, it is not proud.

5 It is not rude, it is not self-seeking, it is not easily angered, it keeps no record of wrongs.

6 Love does not delight in evil but rejoices with the truth.

7 It always protects, always trusts, always hopes, always perseveres.

8 Love never fails. But where there are prophecies, they will cease; where there are tongues, they will be stilled; where there is knowledge, it will pass away.

9 For we know in part and we prophesy in part,

10 but when perfection comes, the imperfect disappears.

11 When I was a child, I talked like a child, I thought like a child, I reasoned like a child. When I became a man, I put childish ways behind me.

12 Now we see but a poor reflection as in a mirror; then we shall see face to face. Now I know in part; then I shall know fully, even as I am fully known.

13 And now these three remain: faith, hope and love. But the greatest of these is love.

EPHESIANS 5: 21–33

*Wives submit to your husbands,
husbands love your wives.*

21 Submit to one another out of reverence
for Christ.

22 Wives, submit to your husbands as to
the Lord.

23 For the husband is the head of the wife
as Christ is the head of the church, his
body, of which he is the Saviour.

24 Now as the church submits to Christ,
so also wives should submit to their
husbands in everything.

25 Husbands, love your wives, just as
Christ loved the church and gave himself
up for her

26 to make her holy, cleansing her by the washing with water through the word,

27 and to present her to himself as a radiant church, without stain or wrinkle or any other blemish, but holy and blameless.

28 In this same way, husbands ought to love their wives as their own bodies. He who loves his wife loves himself.

29 After all, no one ever hated his own body, but he feeds and cares for it, just as Christ does the church –

30 for we are members of his body.

31 'For this reason a man will leave his father and mother and be united to his wife, and the two will become one flesh.'

32 This is a profound mystery – but I am talking about Christ and the church.

33 However, each one of you also must love his wife as he loves himself, and the wife must respect her husband.

1 JOHN 4: 7–12

Beloved, let us love one another.

7 Dear friends, let us love one another, for love comes from God. Everyone who loves has been born of God and knows God.

8 Whoever does not love does not know God, because God is love.

9 This is how God showed his love among us: He sent his one and only Son into the world that we might live through him.

10 This is love: not that we loved God, but that he loved us and sent his Son as an atoning sacrifice for our sins.

11 Dear friends, since God so loved us, we also ought to love one another.

12 No one has ever seen God; but if we love one another, God lives in us and his love is made complete in us.

The marriage of the Lamb.

5 Then a voice came from the throne, saying: 'Praise our God, all you his servants, you who fear him, both small and great!'

6 Then I heard what sounded like a great multitude, like the roar of rushing waters and like loud peals of thunder, shouting: 'Hallelujah! For our Lord God Almighty reigns.

7 Let us rejoice and be glad and give him glory! For the wedding of the Lamb has come, and his bride has made herself ready.

8 Fine linen, bright and clean, was given her to wear.'
9 Then the angel said to me, 'Write: "Blessed are those who are invited to the wedding supper of the Lamb!"' And he added, 'These are the true words of God.'

ADDITIONAL BIBLE READINGS

The following is a list of additional Bible readings that you might like to look up for yourself.

Genesis 9: 8–17 *The rainbow and God's covenant with Noah.*

Joshua 24: 15 *As for me and my house we will serve the Lord.*

Ruth 1: 16–17 *Wither thou goest I will go.*

Psalm 8 *O Lord, how majestic is thy name.*

Psalm 34: 1–3 *Let us exalt his name together.*

ADDITIONAL BIBLE READINGS

Psalm 127 *Unless the Lord builds the house...*
Psalm 136: 1–9 *His steadfast love endures forever.*
Psalm 150 *Praise the Lord!*
Proverbs 3: 1–6, 13–18 *Let not loyalty and faithfulness forsake you.*
Isaiah 30: 21 *This is the way, walk in it.*
Isaiah 32: 2,16–18 *Each will be like a hiding place, like streams in dry land.*
Isaiah 54: 10–14 *My steadfast love will not depart from you.*

ADDITIONAL BIBLE READINGS

Isaiah 61: 10–11 *Clothed in salvation…
as a bride adorns herself with her jewels.*
Jeremiah 33: 10–11 *There will be heard once
more the voices of the bride and bridegroom.*
Hosea 2: 19–20 *I will betroth you to me
forever.*
Matthew 5: 13–16 *You are the light of the
world.*
Matthew 6: 19–21 *Where your treasure is,
there will your heart be also.*

ADDITIONAL BIBLE READINGS

Matthew 7: 24–29 *A wise man built his house upon a rock.*
Romans 12: 9–12 *Let love be genuine.*
Ephesians 3: 14–19 *May you be grounded and rooted in love.*
Colossians 3: 12–17 *Put on love, which binds everything together in harmony.*

LITERARY ACKNOWLEDGMENTS

Permission to quote Kahlil Gibran's poem *On Marriage* and from *The Prophet* was granted by the Gibran National Committee, P.O. Box 116-5375, Beirut, Lebanon; phone and fax: (+961-1) 676916; e-mail: k.gibran@cyberia.net.lb

Permission to quote from *Fidelity*, part of *The Complete Works of D.H. Lawrence*, was granted by Laurence Pollinger Limited and the Estate of Frieda Lawrence Ravagli.

LITERARY ACKNOWLEDGMENTS

ABOUT CONFETTI.CO.UK

Confetti.co.uk is the UK's leading wedding and special occasion website, helping more than 100,000 brides, grooms and guests every month.

To find out more or to order your confetti.co.uk gift book or party brochure, visit www.confetti.co.uk, call 0870 840 6060, or e-mail us at info@confetti.co.uk

Other books in this series include *The Wedding Book of Calm*; *Men at Weddings*; *Compatibility*; *Confettiquette*; *Speeches* and the comprehensive *Wedding Planner*.